Learning a Lesson

How you see, think and remember

Steve Parker

FRANKLIN WATTS
New York • London • Toronto • Sydney

Franklin Watts, Inc.
387 Park Avenue South
New York, NY 10016

Library of Congress Cataloging-in-Publication Data

Parker, Steve.
    Learning a lesson: how you see, think and remember / Steve Parker.
        p.   cm. — (The Body in action)
    Summary: Explains the functions of the brain and nervous system,
and how sensory experiences and information are processed.
    ISBN 0-531-14087-3
    1. Human information processing—Juvenile literature.   2. Senses
and sensation—Juvenile literature.   3. Central nervous system—
Juvenile literature.   [1. Brain.   2. Nervous system.]   I. Title.
II. Series.
QP396.P37   1991
612.8—dc20   89-77860
                                                                CIP AC

Printed in Great Britain

Medical consultant:
Dr. Puran Ganeri, MBBS, MRCP, MRCGP, DCH

Series editor: Anita Ganeri
Design: K and Co.
Illustrations: Hayward Art
Photography: Chris Fairclough
Typesetting: Lineage Ltd, Watford

The publisher would like to thank Anna Ridout for appearing in the
photographs of this book.

CONTENTS

4 The lesson begins

6 The senses

8 The eyes and seeing

11 Brain power

14 Nerve signals

16 Making sense

18 Remembering

20 Understanding

22 The two-sided brain

24 The brain in control

26 Learning to learn

28 Things to do

30 Glossary and resources

32 Index

The lesson begins

Everything you do involves your brain. It is the part of you that thinks, makes decisions, feels emotions, learns and remembers. You don't learn only in lessons at school. All through your life you are taking in new knowledge and learning how to do new things. You learned to eat, smile and walk without realizing it. But other things, such as learning to play a musical instrument, need a lot of effort and hard work.

△ The brain is where the "mind" and memory are. As the lesson begins, you concentrate on storing information in your brain.

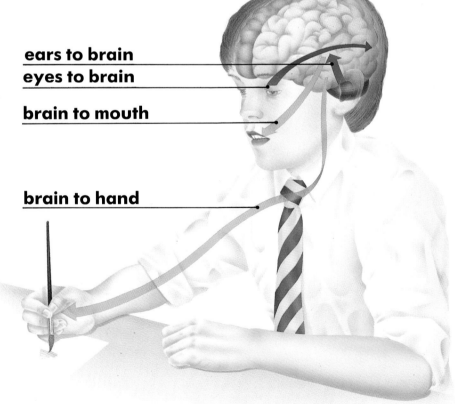

ears to brain

eyes to brain

brain to mouth

brain to hand

▷ Your brain receives information from your eyes and ears. It sends messages to your mouth and hand muscles, so you can speak and draw.

4

HOW LONG ARE MEMORIES?

As you learn, you store information in your brain's memory. But your brain does not store every memory forever. You usually forget little things. Can you remember your first day at school? You probably can — it was very important. But what about your 23rd day? Older people have many years to look back on. They may forget everyday events, such as what they had for lunch. They remember important events, such as wartime, or a wedding. Memories can last for over 50 or 60 years.

DOES IT MAKE SENSE?

The two pictures shown here both have exactly the same numbers and shapes of lines. The only difference is in the way that the lines are arranged. Look at one picture for 10 seconds. Then close the book and try to draw it. Do the same with the other picture. Which one can you remember best? Probably the one on the right, because you recognize it as a human face. Your brain is constantly trying to understand and make sense of the world, by recognizing patterns.

Making sense of something by giving it a "meaning," or pattern, usually makes it easier to remember.

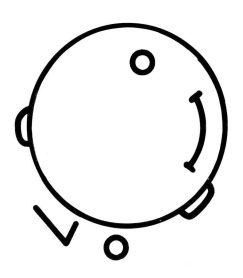

The senses

Your senses tell you what is happening all around you. You have five main sets of sense organs. These are your eyes, ears, nose, tongue and skin. In a flash, these sense organs send nerve messages to your brain, to make you aware of what is happening.

△ Eyes and ears tell you most about the world, but other senses help when needed. The sandwich looks all right on the outside. It also smells delicious, so you know it is good to eat.

▷ Sight, smell, taste and hearing are detected by sense organs in your head. The sense organ for touch is the skin, all over your body. Touch is a "multi-sense" because you can feel pressure and pain, as well as heat and cold.

The brain is in the top half of the head, protected by skull bones.

eyes detect light

ears detect sound

skin detects touch

nose detects smell

tongue detects taste

SENSE FACTS

• Your brain receives millions of messages from your sense organs every second. But it only pays attention to those which are important, such as the smell of burning detected by your nose.
• The body's sense of position is balance. This sense involves gravity and movement detectors in your ears, stretch sensors in your

skin and muscles, and information coming in from your eyes.
• When you are bicycling in traffic, all your senses are busy, and your brain is alert to the slightest risk of danger — such as a person stepping into the street, a police car siren wailing, or the smell of slippery oil which could throw you off balance.

CAN YOU FOLLOW THE CLOCK?

To discover how your ears help you find the position of a sound, try this test. Blindfold a friend, who sits still. Move a ticking clock around her or his head. The sound of the tick reaches each of his or her ears at a slightly different time. The brain senses the difference and so your friend can pinpoint each position of the clock.

The eyes and seeing

Eyesight is your main sense. Your eyes look out at the world from just in front of your brain. They are protected by your eyelids and the curved bones of your skull. They detect a moving picture of your surroundings, in three dimensions and in color. They do this by turning light rays into messages, which travel along nerves to your brain. A large part of your brain is set aside just to deal with messages from your eyes.

△ Sight is very important for gathering information. About four-fifths of the knowledge in your brain enters through your eyes.

▷ Your eye is about an inch wide. It has a tough, flexible outer coat, called the sclera. Light rays enter through a hole, called the pupil. They shine a picture of the world onto more than 130 million tiny light detectors at the back, in the retina.

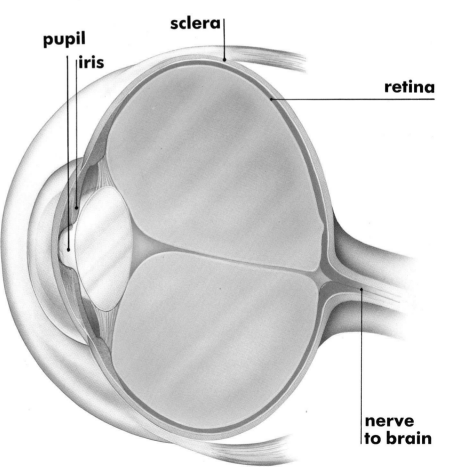

pupil
iris
sclera
retina
nerve to brain

HOW WELL DO YOU SEE COLOR?

Your eye contains three types of detectors for seeing red, yellow-green, and blue-violet colors. In certain people, some detectors do not work properly. This gives a defect of color vision. To test how well you see color, look at the dots in the circles on the right. What numbers can you see in the circles?

5 means normal vision. 2 means a color defect.

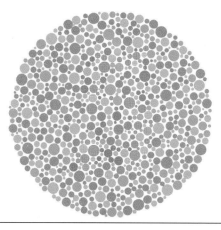

2 means normal vision. No number means a defect.

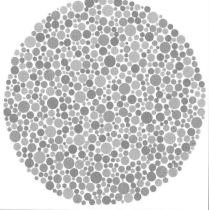

TRICKS OF COLOR

This enlarged part of a picture shows the colored dots.

The pictures in this book may seem to be all the colors of the rainbow. But color printing tricks your eyes. It uses only four inks, or pigments. These are magenta (a red purple), cyan (a type of blue-green), yellow, and black. The inks are printed on the paper in tiny dots of pure color. From a distance, your eye cannot see the separate dots. It merges them together. The proportion of dots of each pigment determines the overall color that you see.

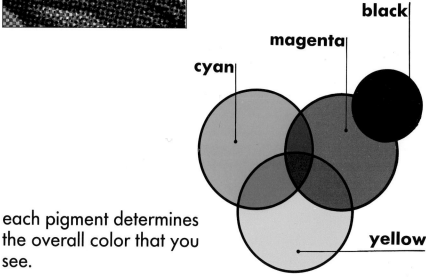

black

magenta

cyan

yellow

9

BELIEVE IT OR NOT!

Seeing is believing, or is it? Your eyes and brain can play tricks. In the picture on the top right, is the square in the circles really bent? In the picture on the far right, which line is longer? Check with a ruler. Each of your eyes also has a blind spot in its retina. This is where the main nerve leaves the eyeball and there are no light detectors. Follow the instructions on the right to test your blind spot.

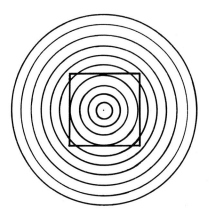

Hold the book 12 inches away, cover your left eye, and stare at the cross.

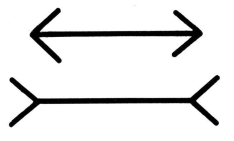

Move the page nearer. When light rays from the black dot fall on your blind spot, the dot disappears.

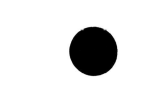

HOW MANY PICTURES?

Your eyes detect light rays and turn them into electrical nerve signals. Your brain sorts these signals and gives them a meaning. Look at the pictures on the right. Your brain realizes there are two pictures here and "jumps" between them, even though only one set of signals comes from your eyes.

◁ Is this the man in the moon, or an old witch?

▽ Is this a young lady with a hat, or an old lady?

Brain power

Your brain is linked to your senses and to all the other parts of your body by nerves. These are microscopically thin "wires" that thread their way around and into all your body parts. They carry nerve messages in the form of tiny electrical signals.

△ You learn things and work out problems in your brain. You use your experience, and information from your senses, such as the shape and color of a jigsaw piece, to guess where it fits.

▷ A long bundle of nerves, called the spinal cord, runs down from the base of your brain. This is the main link from your brain to your body. Nerves from the spinal cord spread out to many parts of your body, from your fingertips to the ends of your toes.

brain

nerves to arms and hands

spinal cord

nerves to heart and lungs

nerves to stomach, intestines and other internal organs

nerves to legs and feet

11

INSIDE YOUR BRAIN

Inside your brain is a vast network of millions of nerves, connected in billions of ways. These connections allow you to think and work out problems, such as where a jigsaw piece fits. You are aware of these kinds of thoughts, and of feelings and emotions, which also happen in your brain.

But your brain does many other jobs which you are not aware of. Every second, it automatically controls dozens of processes inside you. These include breathing, your heart beating, and feeling hungry. Your brain also controls the muscles that make you sit up, walk or run.

YOUR SENSITIVE BRAIN

The largest parts of the brain are two rounded, wrinkled lumps on top. They are called the cerebral hemispheres. This is where thinking and learning happen. The surfaces of the hemispheres look the same all over, but they are not. Each hemisphere is divided into regions, called centers. This side view of the brain shows the five main sensory centers. Each deals with messages coming from one main type of sense organ.

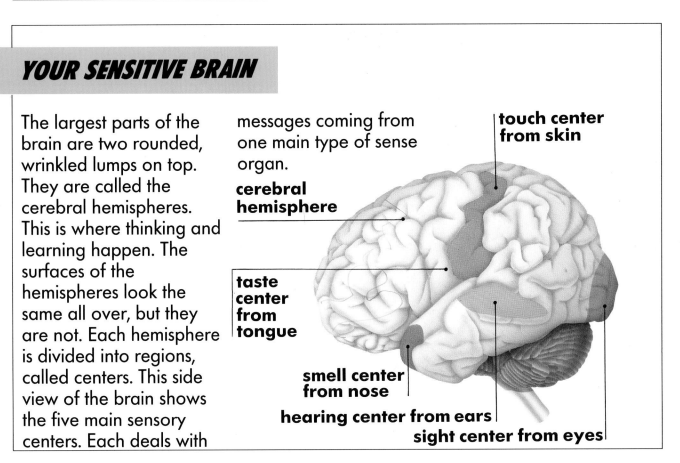

touch center from skin

cerebral hemisphere

taste center from tongue

smell center from nose

hearing center from ears

sight center from eyes

HOW BIG IS YOUR BRAIN?

The brain's cerebral hemispheres have deep folds and grooves. Spread out flat, they would cover an area about the size of a pillowcase! You can see how big they are by taping together six sheets of 8½ x 14 inch writing paper. This is the area of your two cerebral hemispheres.

Now try to bend and fold the sheet so that it is no bigger than the top half of your head!

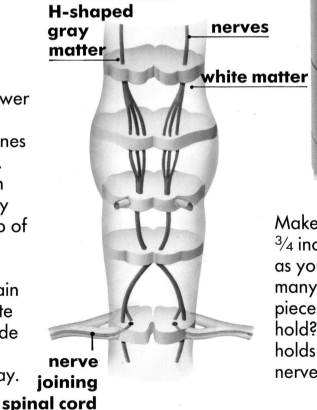

LOOKING AT YOUR SPINAL CORD

The bundle of nerves making up your spinal cord runs inside your backbones, from your brain down to your lower back. Strong joints between your backbones keep the cord straight. Inside, the cord has an H-shaped area of gray matter. This is made up of thousands of nerves carrying messages (impulses) from the brain to your body. The white matter around it is made of nerves carrying messages the other way.

H-shaped gray matter

nerves

white matter

nerve joining spinal cord

Make a cardboard tube ¾ inch across — as thick as your spinal cord. How many drinking straws or pieces of thread does it hold? Your spinal cord holds thousands of nerves!

Nerve signals

Your brain, spinal cord and nerves are made up of billions of nerve cells, called neurons. A neuron is so thin that it can only be seen under a microscope, yet some neurons are many inches long. The nerve message, a tiny electrical signal, travels along the wirelike part of the neuron, called the axon, to the next neuron in the network.

△ When you bang your knee, nerve signals pass from your knee through neurons to your brain, where you feel the pain!

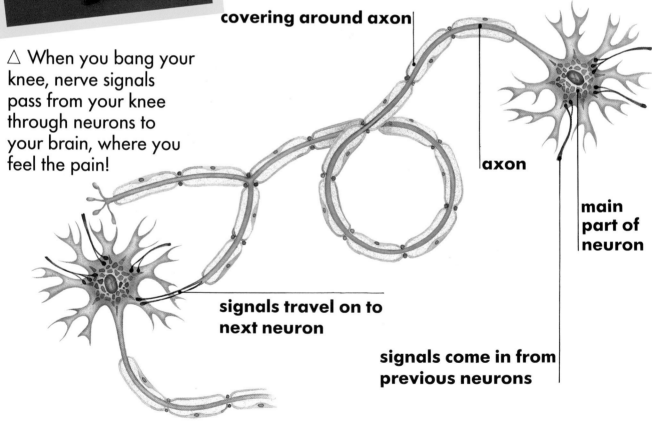

covering around axon

axon

main part of neuron

signals travel on to next neuron

signals come in from previous neurons

△ This is an enlarged view of a nerve cell, or neuron.

NERVE FACTS

- Neurons do not actually touch each other. There are tiny gaps between them, called synapses. Nerve messages "jump" across these gaps from one neuron to the next.
- The longest neurons are 3 feet or more in length. They connect your feet to the lower parts of your spinal cord.
- Messages about a light touch on your skin travel to your brain at a speed of 164 feet per second.
- Messages about a slight pain, such as a pinprick, travel to your brain at about 33 feet per second.
- Messages about more severe pain, such as a stubbed toe, go at 3-6½ feet per second.
- This is why, when you stub your toe, you feel the touch first — and the pain follows a fraction of a second later!

HOW GOOD ARE YOUR REFLEXES?

You cannot be aware of everything, all the time. So your body has automatic reactions, or reflexes, in case of danger. In a reflex action, the body part reacts and moves right away. It does not need messages from your brain. You can test your knee-jerk reflex by sitting with your legs crossed and your knees bent. With the side of your hand, tap just under your knee cap. Does your lower leg "kick" out? Can you keep it from kicking?

(5) A split second later, danger signals travel to brain.

(2) Sensor sends nerve signals to spinal cord.

(1) Stretch sensor in knee warns that leg is bending.

(3) Reflex connection in spinal cord sends signals onwards.

(4) Signals travel back to leg muscles and straighten leg.

Making sense

Getting information into your brain from your senses is only part of learning. Your brain has to sort out all the information. It has to decide what to remember, what to forget, whether it must tell the body to take any action, and what it understands (see page 20). All these processes take place in the form of nerve signals, flashing around the huge network of neurons inside your brain.

△ A computer is like a very simplified brain. Electrical signals travel back and forth, and are sorted out by the computer's central processor.

neuron

connection to next neuron

◁ Just a few neurons make a complex maze of connections. A nerve signal could follow many different paths. Some neurons are joined to 200,000 others!

THINKING LOGICALLY

Your brain can work through a problem, step by step, to find an answer. We call this "reasoning," or "logical thought" (see page 22). This kind of thinking is important in games, such as chess. There are six types of chess pieces, and each moves only in a certain

pawn
knight
bishop
rook

way. A good chess player works out what might happen if any piece is moved, and tries to plan the game several moves in advance.
The other two pieces are the king and the queen.

HOW LOGICAL ARE YOU?

Logical thought helps you to solve puzzles such as finding a way through a maze. But sometimes your brain "jumps" to the answer right away. Look at the two mazes on the right. Can you see at once the correct paths through them? Next, try to connect all three houses to the water, gas and electricity supplies. Draw in the pipes and wires, but be careful. They are not allowed to cross! (The answer is on page 31.)

maze 1

maze 2

house 1   **house 2**   **house 3**

gas   **electricity**   **water**

Remembering

During a lesson, you look, listen and try to learn, so that you can remember afterward. The first part of the memory process is putting information into your brain's memory. The second stage is remembering, or getting information out again. But what is a "memory?" A single memory may exist as a pattern of connections between neurons. Nerve messages travel around this pattern and make a "circuit" in the network.

△ A computer, like your brain, has a memory. The computer's memory is usually a pattern of tiny patches of magnetism on a tape or disk.

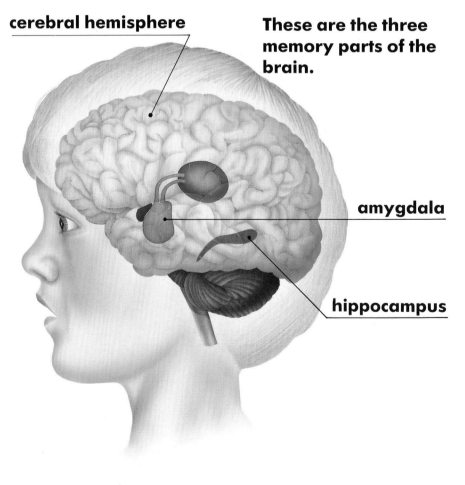

cerebral hemisphere

These are the three memory parts of the brain.

amygdala

hippocampus

▷ For years, scientists have tried to find the brain's "memory center." But it seems that memories are not stored in one place. They are spread through many parts of the brain, as shown on the right.

18

MEMORY FACTS

● Some people have a "photographic" memory. They can remember what a page of writing looks like, without reading it. They then remember the words by calling up a "photograph" of the page.

● It is often easier to remember something from a clue. You may not be able to draw a friend's face from memory. But you could recognize her or his hair, eyes and nose from an "identikit" set of features. You could put these together to make a good likeness.

● One memory expert remembered 612 playing cards in order, after seeing them only once. He made only four mistakes.

● Most people's memory will get better with practice. In one test, a person practiced remembering different groups of numbers, each day. After 50 days, his score had gone up from 80 to 120.

HOW GOOD IS YOUR MEMORY?

Test your memory by looking at the objects in the picture below, for 15 seconds. Then look away and try to write down the names of as many objects as possible. You will probably find that you do better if you use a memory trick of some kind (see pages 20-21).

For example, take the first letters of the names of each object and try to make a word from them, like "PAWCOT."

Understanding

△ You cannot learn if you are daydreaming or if your attention wanders. You need to concentrate on understanding and remembering the main parts of the lesson.

When your brain receives and sorts out messages, it needs to make sense of them and understand them. It is easier to learn and remember things if they have a pattern you can recognize, as shown below.

1 SEEING

Your eyes see these lines and squiggles, and send messages to your brain about them. But they are difficult to remember, because they have no meaning. You cannot understand them.

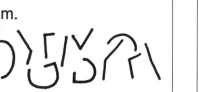

2 RECOGNIZING

These are the same lines as before, but rearranged into letters which you can recognize. However, they do not spell a word. They would be easier to remember if they had a meaning.

3 UNDERSTANDING

The letters are the first letters of each of the colors in a rainbow, in the correct order. They are Red, Orange, Yellow, Green, Blue, Indigo, Violet. Now the words have a meaning.

4 REMEMBERING

You can remember the colors of the rainbow by a simple "learning trick." Use the first letter in each color's name to make the boy's name Roy G. Biv. This has nothing to do with rainbows, but it is a name which will spark a memory of the rainbow colors.

LEARN TO REMEMBER

The main notes in music are A, B, C, D, E, F and G. These are easy to remember as the first seven letters of the alphabet. But when writing music on the staves, which notes go on the lines or in the gaps? Try these two "learning tricks" to help you recall which notes go where.

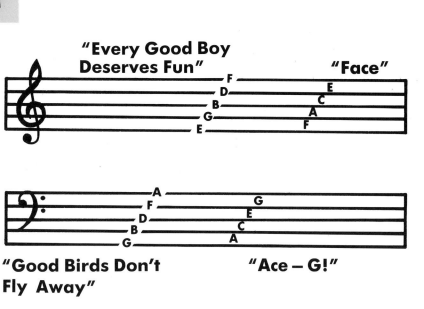

"Every Good Boy Deserves Fun"

"Face"

"Good Birds Don't Fly Away"

"Ace – G!"

TYPES OF MEMORY

Short-term memory works for seconds or a few minutes. You might use it for a telephone number, between looking up the number in the book and dialing.

Medium-term memory lasts for a few days or weeks. You might use it to remember the time of a visit to the dentist or the day you have an examination at school.

Long-term memory lasts for years. You can recall names, places, and also how to do things. Even if you have not tied shoe-laces for many years, you can usually do it the first time when you try again.

The two-sided brain

The two sides of your brain look similar, but there are differences between them. In most people, the left side of the brain deals more with "logical" thought (see page 17), such as working out sums. The right side deals mainly with creative and artistic abilities. It tends to leap right to an answer or idea.

LEFT SIDE
logic and planning
chess and similar games
speech
maths
computer programming

RIGHT SIDE
creative abilities
music
painting
dance
emotions
recognizing shapes and patterns

△ When you are doing something creative, such as playing a musical instrument, your brain's right side is usually in charge.

▷ The two sides of your brain are connected by a thick "strap" of nerves, called the corpus callosum. It allows them to exchange nerve messages. It has more than 200 million neurons, and does not form fully until you are about 10 years old.

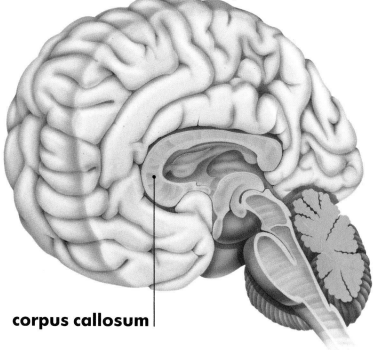

corpus callosum

BRAIN FACTS

- The average human brain weighs about 3-3¼ pounds. It takes up ¹⁄₅₀ of the total body weight.
- A gorilla's brain takes up about ¹⁄₁₅₀ of its body weight.
- The giant dinosaur Stegosaurus had a tiny brain. Its brain took up about ¹⁄₂₀₀,₀₀₀ of its body weight!
- About 11 out of every 100 people are left-handed. They use their left hand for playing music, drawing and so on.

WRITING WITH THE WRONG HAND

As you grow older, your writing and drawing abilities get better. But these skills are like many others — you improve with help, teaching and practice. Also, your brain and body get used to doing movements in a certain way. These words were written by children using their usual hand, and then with the other hand. Try this for yourself. You will soon see how difficult it is to use the other hand! A few people are equally skilled with either hand. They are called ambidextrous.

The cat Sat on the mat.

normal writing of left-hander

The cat Sat on the mat

left-hander using right hand

Alan parker age 9 left handed

Thorndon primary school

normal writing of right-hander

Browenton primary school

right-hander using left hand

Tim welch age 9 right handed.

23

The brain in control

Every movement your body makes is powered by your muscles. But muscles only work when your brain tells them to. A special part of your brain, called the motor center, deals with sending out messages along nerves to your muscles. The motor center is a long strip running down each side of your brain. Different parts of the strip control different muscles.

△ The brain controls movement and also staying still. Using your sense of balance, you learn to tense your muscles by just the right amount as you stand on one foot, to keep you from falling over.

▷ Different parts of the brain control movement in the body. The colored areas (above right) show which parts.

▷ The motor center on the left side of the brain controls muscles on the right side of the body. The motor center on the right side controls muscles on the left of the body.

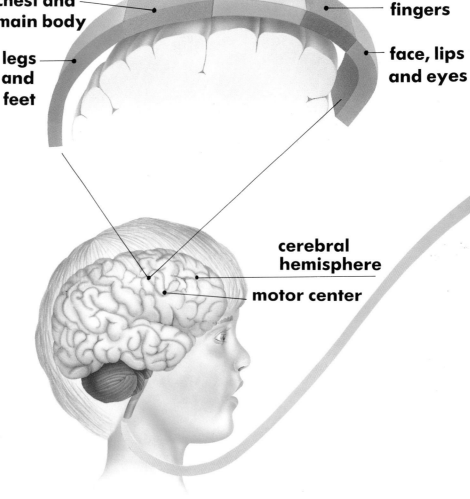

chest and
main body

arm and hand

fingers

legs
and
feet

face, lips
and eyes

cerebral
hemisphere

motor center

LEARNING NEW MOVEMENTS

Try teaching your body some new movements. Hold a pencil in each hand, with their points facing each other. Keeping one pencil still, move the other in a circle in the air. Now draw circles with both pencils, but move them in opposite directions. They should meet halfway around, and again when they have come full circle. This may be hard to do at first! Keep trying for a few minutes and you will get better.

Nerve signals travel along nerve in arm.

Signals control hand muscles when writing.

◁ When you decide to move a part of your body, the motor center sends nerve messages out along your spinal cord and nerves, to the correct muscles. When the messages arrive they make your muscles move. Writing is a complicated skill involving dozens of muscles. They work together to make many tiny movements.

25

Learning to learn

You cannot learn everything. At school, you cannot learn the name of every country in the world. You cannot memorize the answer to every math problem. But you can learn basic rules about how to do something. You can learn how to look up the names of countries in an atlas. You can learn the rules about how to add or multiply numbers. By following simple rules, you can work out the answers to difficult problems.

△ Some people are able to draw well from an early age. But most people can learn to draw or paint, with teaching and practice. Learning like this is important, as well as learning facts.

▷ These drawings were done by children of different ages. See how the children get better at drawing as they get older. Try drawing a car or dog yourself. How do you compare?

4 years

8 years

12 years

LEARNING FACTS

- You learn all through your life.
- As a baby, you learned to sit up, then crawl, and then walk.
- You continue to learn about movements, coordination and balance, such as when you learn to thread a needle or ride a bicycle.
- You learn to recognize. You know people you see every day, like your family and friends. But would you recognize a relative that you have not seen for two years? Would you recognize your new coat in the school lost and found box?
- You learn to get along with others and make friends.

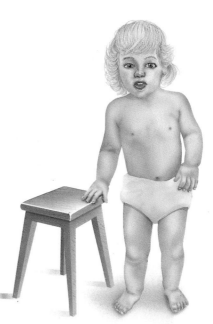

GIVING YOUR BRAIN A BREAK

You cannot keep concentrating and learning for hours at a time. Thinking takes energy. This is why you have breaks between lessons at school. A break helps you to relax and become refreshed. It is also difficult to think or learn properly if your brain is too tired, from lack of sleep. Caring for your brain and mind is just as important as keeping your muscles fit and healthy.

SCHOOL SCHEDULE	9:30 10:15	10:20 11:00	11:05 11:45	12:00 12:45	
MON	Math	English	P.E.		LUNCH
TUES	Art	Science	Music		
WED	French	Math	History		

Things to do

MEMENTOS

Memories often seem to fade away, but then they are brought back by an object, such as a photograph or a piece of clothing. We often call these objects mementos, because they help us to remember. Do you have any mementos? Do older members of your family have any? What do they help you to remember?

REMEMBERING TO REMEMBER

You may need to remember something for a short time. But you might forget it, and you may also forget that you are supposed to remember anything at all! It helps if you have a memory "trigger." One way to do this is to tie a small piece of string around your finger. Each time you see or feel the string, it reminds you that you must remember something. Then you can start to think about what the "something" is.

SORTING THROUGH YOUR MEMORY

You can sort through your memory to find what you want, in a similar way to sorting through the books in a library. Consider this question: How many windows are there in your house? You probably do not know right away. But think about it. In your "mind's eye," you can walk into a room in your house and see how many windows there are. Do this for every room, adding up the windows as you go, and you'll get the answer.

CHANGING WHAT YOU REMEMBER

Try to remember these shapes by giving each one a "label." For example, the left one could be a pine tree, the middle one a number 7, and the right one a beehive. Write out the labels (but not the shapes). After a couple of hours, look at the labels again, but not the shapes, and try to draw the shapes from memory. Compare your drawings with the original shapes. Have you remembered them exactly? Or has each shape become more like the objects you imagine from your "labels?"

LEFT AND RIGHT

Try to move your fingers apart and back together in two pairs. Do it several times. Is it easy, or do you have to concentrate? Which hand did you try with? Probably your right one if you are right-handed, or the left one if you are left-handed. Now try the same movement with the other hand. Is it more difficult? Most people learn to carry out complicated tasks, such as writing or painting, with mainly one hand. Try some tasks with the hand you do not usually use. Can you cut up your food with your knife and fork in the "wrong hands?" What about tying your shoelaces by making each hand do the movements that the other one would normally do?

MORE PRACTICE

You can carry out all sorts of movements — with practice. Stand still and try to pat your head with one hand, and at the same time rub your tummy with your other hand. Most people cannot do this the first time they try. But practice for a few minutes. Do you get better? Is it then easier to learn to rub your head and pat your tummy instead?

Glossary

Brain A large, tangled mass of interconnected nerves inside the head. It is the control center of the body. Other nerves link it to the various body parts.

Center A specialized part of the brain which deals with nerve messages coming in from, or going out to, a certain part of the body. For example, the hearing center deals with nerve messages coming from the ear.

Forgetting "Un-remembering," when you can no longer recall something that you once knew.

Learning Gaining the ability to say or do something which you were not able to do before, usually in the form of knowledge or a physical skill. It varies from learning to walk as a baby, to learning the name of your hometown, to learning to fly a jet plane.

Logical thought Thinking that involves step-by-step reasoning, each step following from the last, such as figuring out where to put your X in a game of tic-tac-toe.

Motor center The part of the brain specialized in sending out nerve messages to the muscles. It controls many of the body's movements.

Muscle Part of the body that can contract, or get shorter. As it does so it pulls on other parts, such as bones or other muscles, and moves them.

Nerve A long, thin bundle of neurons (nerve cells) that carries nerve messages from one part of the body to another.

Nerve message A series of tiny bursts of electricity, called impulses, that travel along a nerve, like electrical signals going along a telephone wire.

Neuron A single nerve cell, which is so thin that it can only be seen under a microscope.

Resources

Pain A feeling of strong discomfort, hurt or distress. It usually warns that something is wrong with the body.

Remembering The brain's ability to store knowledge, thoughts, feelings, movements, skills and other information, and recall it again at a later time.

Sense organ A part of the body that detects some aspect of its surroundings, turns it into electrical nerve messages, and sends these to the brain. The eye does this with light rays.

United States Government Printing Office
Superintendent of Documents
Washington, D.C. 20402

(Request leaflets on classroom skills, health and fitness)

BOOKS TO READ

Every Kid's Guide to Thinking and Learning
by Joy Berry.
Chicago; Children's Press, 1987.

Memory Skills **by S. Read.**
Tulsa; EDC Publishing, 1988.

The Brain and Nervous System **by Steve Parker.**
New York; Franklin Watts, 1990.

It's All in Your Head: A Guide to Understanding Your Brain and Boosting Your Brain Power
by Susan L. Barrett.
Minneapolis; Free Spirit Pub. Co., 1985.

The Human Body and How it Works
by Angela Royston.
New York; Warwick, 1991.

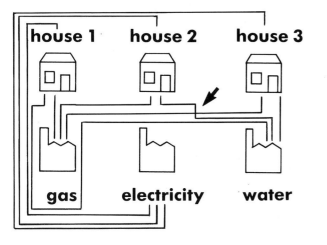

Answer
Page 17   The house puzzle cannot be done. Most people get within one connection of solving the puzzle. But the last connection has to cross another line, as you can see here.

Index

ambidextrous people 23
amygdala 18
axon 14

backbones 13
balance 7, 24, 27
blind spot 10
body 11, 13, 15, 23, 25, 30, 31
bones 6, 8, 13, 30
brain 4, 5, 6, 7, 8, 10, 11-13, 14,
    15, 16, 20, 24, 30
        two sides 22-23
        weight 23
breathing 12

center 12, 24-25, 30
cerebral hemispheres 12, 13, 18,
    24
color vision 8, 9
computer 16, 18, 22
coordination 27
corpus callosum 22
creative abilities 22

ears 4, 6, 7, 12, 30
electrical signals 10, 11, 14, 16, 30,
    31
eyes 4, 6, 7, 8-10, 12, 20, 31

forgetting 5, 16, 30

gray matter 13

hearing 6, 12, 30
head 6, 7, 30
heart 11
heartbeat 12
hippocampus 18

knee-jerk reflex 15

learning 4, 16, 21, 25, 26-27, 30
left-handed people 23, 29
light detectors 8, 9, 10
light rays 8, 10, 31
logical thought 17, 22, 30
long-term memory 21
lungs 11

medium-term memory 21
memories 5, 28
memory 4, 5, 18, 19, 21, 28
messages 4, 7, 8, 11, 12, 13, 14,
    15, 20, 24, 25, 30
mind 4
motor center 24-25, 30
mouth 4
movement 24-25, 27, 30
movement detectors 7
muscles 4, 7, 12, 15, 24, 25, 27, 30

nerve cells 14, 30
nerve connections 12
nerve messages 4, 6, 7, 11, 15, 18,
    22, 30, 31
nerve signals 10, 14-15, 16, 25
nerves 8, 10, 11, 13, 14, 20, 22,
    24, 25, 30
neurons 14, 15, 16, 18, 22, 30
nose 6, 7, 12

pain 6, 14, 15, 31
patterns 5
pigments 9
pressure 6
pupil 8

reasoning 17, 30
recognizing 20, 22, 27
reflex actions 15
remembering 5, 16, 18-19, 20, 28,
    29, 31
retina 8, 10
right-handed people 23, 29

sclera 8
seeing 20
sense organs 6-7, 12, 31
senses 6-7, 8, 11, 16
sensory centers 12
short-term memory 21
sight 6, 12
skin 6, 7, 12, 15
skull 6, 8
smell 6, 7, 12
sound 6, 7
spinal cord 11, 13, 14, 15, 25
stretch sensors 7, 15
synapses 15

taste 6, 12
tongue 6, 12
touch 6, 12, 15

understanding 16, 20-21

white matter 13

02